Me and You, Lord

By Susan Tosounian
Illustrated by Amanda Paschal

Copyright © 2017 Susan Tosounian
All rights reserved.

This book or any portion thereof may not be reproduced or used in any manner whatsoever without the express written permission of the publisher except for the use of brief quotations in a book review.

ISBN-13: 978-0692963623
ISBN-10: 0692963626
Library of Congress Control Number: 2017915600
Front cover image by Amanda Paschal
Book design by Liasco Press
Printed in the United States of America
First Printing, 2017
Published by Liasco Press
Los Angeles, CA
liascopress@gmail.com

Thank you to:

My Lord and Savior

Artin, who is always my #1 fan

Liana + Sasco Joe, who inspired this book and who are God's daily love warriors

David + Henry, my genius nephews

Shannon Cirricione, who teaches as much out of the classroom as she does in it.

About Me And You, Lord…

Prayer is personal conversation directly with God. You can talk with God about anything, anytime!

The purpose of this book is to support growth in each reader's relationship with God through prayer. Each prayer is designed for personalization by the child, encouraging the child to be more thoughtful in prayer, opening the heart to the truth that God truly is there for each and every one of us.

There is a Parent's Corner on each page that provides a conversation starter related to the prayer, fostering bond-strengthening discussion between parent(s) and child.

We have provided Word Boxes at the end of the book that have various Nouns, Adjectives and Verbs that younger children can choose from if they need a little help to find a word when they are at a loss for it. There is also a table of Biblical role models to read about, in the event your child is interested in exploring regular people like us being used for God's glory.

May this book be a blessing to all.

Proverbs 22:6 (NIV) Start children off on the way they should go, and even when they are old they will not turn from it.

Me and You, Lord

My Lord,

You are my (NOUN). I know that You are with me every day. When things feel out of control, You gently (VERB) me.

I know that You are in control and that makes me feel (ADJECTIVE). I trust You and I (VERB) You. There is nothing that can take away Your love for me. Help me to glorify You every day when I (VERB) with my friends. I'm so thankful for the love, forgiveness and strength You always give me.

In Jesus' name I pray,

Amen

Parent's corner

Ask your child to share a time when things felt out of control (on the playground, with homework, with a sibling) and what it felt like.

Dear God,

Thank you Lord for my [ADJECTIVE] family. Today, I want to say a special prayer for my [FAMILY MEMBER]. I pray that he/she always feels [ADJECTIVE]. I love that he/she [VERB ENDING IN S] with me. Lord, work in my heart so I am more [ADJECTIVE] to him/her so that I share the love You have given me. I pray that we grow closer to You every day.

In Jesus' name I pray,

Amen

Parent's corner

Ask your child why he/she chose this particular family member for this prayer. Share something you love about the family member he/she chose.

I will be a Father to you, and you will be my sons and daughters, says the Lord Almighty
2 Corinthians 6:18 (NIV)

My Heavenly Father,

Thank you God for today. It was a (ADJECTIVE) day.

Thank You for my (ALL FAMILY MEMBERS). I know You always listen when I pray. Today I pray that my family always remembers that You (VERB) us. I know that You smile when we (VERB) together. It makes me smile too! I know we make mistakes and are sometimes (ADJECTIVE) to each other, but You love us and forgive us. We want to follow Your example in everything we do. Help us to remember that we are family and help us to forgive each other when we are feeling (ADJECTIVE).

We love You and want to be more like You.

In Jesus' name I pray,

Amen

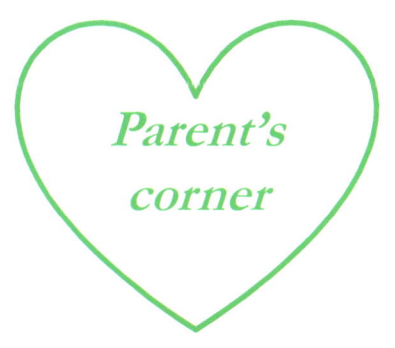

Parent's corner

Share a family memory that you know made God smile. Then, share a time when you experienced forgiveness in your family and discuss how it made you feel after you received or gave forgiveness.

God Almighty,

Thank You for my friend (FRIEND'S NAME).

We are always (VERB ENDING IN -ING) together.

He/She makes me feel (ADJECTIVE). When (FRIEND'S NAME) feels (ADJECTIVE), I pray that You bless him/her with (NOUN). I want to be a good friend to him/her and I ask that You bless our friendship so that we can be there for each other on good days and bad days.

In Jesus' name I pray,

Amen

Parent's corner

Let your child know that having good friends is a blessing. Ask your child what makes a good friend.

Dear Lord,

Thank You for all the blessings in my life. Today, I want to say a special prayer for my teacher, (TEACHER'S NAME).

Lord, please cover (TEACHER'S NAME) with (NOUN) when he/she is teaching the class. He/She works so hard to teach us all the things we need to learn. (TEACHER'S NAME) is a blessing to us all. Help me be the best student I can be to make him/her (ADJECTIVE). Thank You God for my teacher!

In Jesus' name I pray,

Amen

Let your child know that you will say a special prayer for the teacher tonight and ask your child how that makes him/her feel.

Dear Heavenly Father,

Thank You God for sending Jesus to save me and everyone who believes. You love me so much! Today, I was so excited to come home and see (PET'S NAME). I love how he/she (VERB ENDING IN S) when he/she sees me. Thank You for blessing me with him/her. I pray that You work in my heart to be more (ADJECTIVE) to (PET'S NAME).

He/she deserves all the (NOUN) I can give him/her.

In Jesus' name I pray,

Amen

Parent's corner

Share a memory you have with your childhood pet and how you feel blessed to have had him/her in your life. Brainstorm with your child for an activity you can do with your pet together to create a new memory.

And God said, "Let the land produce living creatures according to their kinds: the livestock, the creatures that move along the ground, and the wild animals, each according to its kind." And it was so.

Genesis 1:24 (NIV)

Dear Lord,

Thank You for all You have given me. Today, I want to say a special prayer for people I don't know. Lord, I pray that everyone knows You and (VERB ENDING IN S) You. I know that You love everybody. I hope they feel the same love You give me.

So many people do not have simple things like (NOUN).

It is amazing that everyone is made in Your image and is Your beautiful creation. I (VERB) You always and thank You for the eternal life You give to those who believe.

In Jesus' name I pray,

Amen

Parent's corner

Let your child know of a group of people that you don't know personally, but that you pray for.

Dear God,

Thank You for being my (NOUN). Lord, You made me unique. I know I am Your child. Help me be the best person I can be! The fruits of the Spirit are: love, joy, peace, patience, kindness, gentleness and self-control. Today, the fruit of the Spirit I pray You help me with is (FRUIT OF THE SPIRIT). I want all my family and friends to be blessed by my fruit of the Spirit. It's all because of You. You are (ADJECTIVE)!

In Jesus' name I pray,

Amen

Ask your child why he/she chose the fruit of the Spirit that he/she chose.

Dear Heavenly Father,

Today is a sad day, Lord. I am [ADJECTIVE] that [PET'S NAME] died. He/She was so [ADJECTIVE]. I loved it when we [VERB ENDING IN ED] together. I am going to miss [PET'S NAME] so much. I pray that You help me to always remember my good memories with [PET'S NAME]. Thank You God for always being with me. I know that You loved [PET'S NAME] too.

In Jesus' name I pray,

Amen

Parent's corner

Share a time when you lost a childhood pet and how you felt. Have a special ceremony to properly say 'Goodbye' to your child's pet.

Dear God,

I am so thankful for everything. Lord, the world is so big and You have made everything in it. Your creations are ___ADJECTIVE___.

The big oceans and the tiny bugs are all made by You. Help me remember to treat the world You created with respect and care. Father, bless the world and all the ___NOUN___ in it.

In Jesus' name I pray,

Amen

Parent's corner

Discuss why it's so important for everyone to respect all of God's creations that share this world with us.

Dear Lord,

I have so much to be thankful for. You protect me and take care of me. Today, I don't feel so well. My **NOUN** hurts. I'm going to get lots of rest so I feel better soon. God, I pray that You heal me so I can **VERB**. I know that I can count on You because You are **ADJECTIVE**. I know so many Bible stories about You healing very sick people. I'm so thankful for the care my **FAMILY MEMBER** is giving me right now. I appreciate it. Thank you God for all my blessings.

In Jesus' name I pray,

Amen

Parent's corner

Share with your child a time that you didn't feel well and how you felt God's comfort. Hug your child to extend God's love for him/her.

My Shepherd,

God, You are good. I love the family You have blessed me with. Today, I pray for my **FAMILY MEMBER**. I love that he/she makes me **ADJECTIVE**. I know that You give him/her **NOUN** when he/she needs it most. Sometimes, he/she worries about things like **NOUN**, but I know that You are in control. You are our King! Thank you God for my **FAMILY MEMBER**.

In Jesus' name I pray,

Amen

Ask your child what his/her favorite trait is of the family member chosen for this prayer.

Dear God,

I feel Your love in my heart every day. Today, I want to pray for someone who hurt my feelings. His/Her name is [PERSON'S NAME]. Maybe [PERSON'S NAME] does not feel [ADJECTIVE] on some days. God, please work in his/her life and help [PERSON'S NAME] feel the joy that only comes when we know You and Your love for us. Lord, I want to forgive [PERSON'S NAME] for hurting my feelings.

It's not easy, but I pray You work in my heart so I can forgive others like You forgive me.

In Jesus' name I pray,

Amen

Parent's corner

Ask your child if he/she can remember a time that he/she hurt someone's feelings. How did it feel after? Did he/she apologize? If so, how did it feel after the apology?

Be kind and compassionate to one another, forgiving each other, just as in Christ God forgave you.
Ephesians 4:32 (NIV)

My Father in Heaven,

Thank You Lord for my friend [FRIEND'S NAME]. I want to say a prayer for [FRIEND'S NAME] today. When it's a tough day, he\she needs help to feel [ADJECTIVE]. I know that You watch over all of us and it makes me happy.

[FRIEND'S NAME] and I are [ADJECTIVE] friends.

Thank You God for choosing [FRIEND'S NAME] to be a friend that I can share things with. I pray that he/she feels the same way.

In Jesus' name I pray,

Amen

Parent's corner

Tell your child how long you've been friends with a friend of yours. Share how your friendship makes you feel. Try to choose a friend that your child knows.

My Father,

Lord, sometimes I am afraid to (VERB). I am scared that other people will think I am (ADJECTIVE). I want to be strong. I don't want to feel scared because I know that You (VERB) me. It was scary when You sent Your Son to die for me, but You did it so that I never have to feel scared or alone. Father, please help me have the courage to face my fears. I know I can be brave with You to help me. I can do all things through You.

In Jesus' name I pray,

Amen

Share a time the Lord helped you when you were afraid. Let your child know that we are all afraid sometimes, but we can always trust in Him.

Dear Lord,

Thank You God Almighty for today. It was (ADJECTIVE)!

I'm so thankful for my pet and I want to say a special prayer for (PET'S NAME). I pray that You bless him/her with (NOUN) because I know that You love all Your creations and (PET'S NAME) is one of them! I love it when we (VERB) together and I'd like to spend more time with him/her and I ask that You work in my heart to make that a priority.

In Jesus' name I pray,

Amen

Let your child know two things that you love most about your family pet that this prayer is for. Ask your child what he/she loves most about the family pet.

Dear Lord,

Thank You God for loving me. Today is special. My feelings have been hurt, but I come to You so I can be strong and forgiving like You are. I'd like to pray for the person who hurt my feelings. His/Her name is ⟨PERSON'S NAME⟩. He/she hurt my feelings by ⟨VERB ENDING IN ING⟩ at me. It didn't feel good. I pray that You bless him/her so he/she doesn't want to ⟨VERB⟩ me or anyone else anymore. I ask that he/she feels ⟨NOUN⟩ in his/her heart. Lord, I want to be like You. Help me to love ⟨PERSON'S NAME⟩ like You love me. In Jesus' name I pray,

Amen

Ask your child to think of a time when he/she did something hurtful and needed forgiveness. Remind your child that adults need forgiveness too!

Dear Shepherd,

Thank You for loving me. Today, I especially want to pray for people I don't know. I don't know everyone, but You do. I pray that everyone accepts You as their Savior. Lord, bless these people with (NOUN) and (NOUN) because You know what they need most. I pray that people feel loved by knowing You are with them. Lord, we are never alone because You always (VERB) us. God, use me to help other people feel safe and happy by using the special talents You gave me to bless people in my community. Thank you God for being my (NOUN)!

In Jesus' name I pray,

Amen

Parent's corner

Ask your child why he/she thinks it's important to pray for people we don't know.

A new command I give you: Love one another. As I have loved you, so you must love one another.
John 13:34 (NIV)

Dear God,

Thank You for my teacher, [TEACHER'S NAME].

I pray that You bless him/her with [NOUN] in his/her life at school and out of school. [TEACHER'S NAME] is an example of Your [NOUN]. I love that You have blessed him/her with being so [ADJECTIVE]. I know it is so hard to teach my class and I think he/she is the best teacher. God, please give [TEACHER'S NAME] the joy and peace that comes with knowing that You are our Savior. My teacher's gift to teach is from You.

In Jesus' name I pray,

Amen

Affirm the importance of the teacher's role in your child's education and life. Express one trait you appreciate about the teacher.

Almighty God,

You are King! One of the ways I feel Your love is through my family. My family makes me think of Your love for me when we (VERB) together. I pray that You continue to (VERB) us. My family and I want You to be (ADJECTIVE) when we spend time together. You are our Heavenly Father, and we worship You together. Thank You for loving us. I pray that You help us (VERB) each other, so that we can love like You as a family. I want my family to always do everything for Your glory.

In Jesus' name I pray,

Amen

Let your child know how you feel blessed by your family, and specify one characteristic of your child that is a blessing to you.

Nouns:

school	home	happiness
food	water	love
fish	clothes	shelter
vacation	friend	warrior
life	sadness	hunger
grace	family	pet
nature	world	earth
ocean	mountains	sky
clouds	flowers	rivers
lakes	fields	prairies
mercy	Church	playground
heart	life	heaven
mom	dad	parents
brother	sister	siblings
grandma	grandpa	provider
aunt	uncle	neighbor
cousin	wisdom	power
protection	healing	eyes
nose	smile	hair
health	patience	strength
kindness	song	hero

Adjectives:

happy	sad	angry
tired	hungry	sweet
loving	lovely	mean
rude	best	worst
awesome	safe	proud
wonderful	kind	patient
nice	small	big
giant	brave	strong
weak	heavy	light
careful	thankful	pleased
eternal	blessed	mad
faithful	good	slow
afraid	hurt	upset

Verbs:

laugh	play	cry
feed	sleep	love
push	work	study
hug	watch	protect
care	eat	jump
bless	cook	learn
worship	smile	guide
heal	walk	run
skip	hop	listen
talk	touch	encourage

Person	What We Can Learn	Bible Passage
Abraham	Obedience, respect, and faithfulness to God	Genesis 22:1-19
Noah	Patience, perseverance, faithfulness, obedience, trust in God's covenant, and endurance	Genesis 6:11-22
Solomon	Wisdom; seeking God; God honors those who honor Him; God will equip us to accomplish the tasks He calls us to if we rely on Him	1 Kings 3:6-15
Daniel	Honoring God with our choices; faithfulness, trust, obedience; devotion to prayer at all times; integrity	Daniel 1:1-21; Daniel 6
Jonah	Repentance; obedience; God is in control, God's compassion; people can change	Jonah
David	Praising God; respect; faith and courage; friendship; honoring God; praising God for all our blessings	Psalm 19; 1 Samuel 17; 1 Chronicles 28:20; 1 Samuel 18:1; Psalm 103

Joshua	leadership; trusting God; obedience; strength and courage; God is faithful to His promises	Joshua 1:1-18, Joshua 1:9; Joshua 5:13-Joshua 6:27
Gideon	Humility; faithfulness; seeking God's will	Judges 6; Judges 8:23
John the Baptist	Preparing the way for people to know Jesus; God has a purpose for each of our lives; faithfulness	Matthew 3:11; John 1:23; John 1:29; Isaiah 40:3-5; Mark 6:14-29
Peter	Forgiveness; God is always working on us; God corrects us out of love; we are always growing in Christ; God will use us for His glory	Luke 22:31-32, John 21:7-19; Matthew 14:22-32; Matthew 16:13-28
Paul	Redemption; God's grace; every person matters to God; humility; being a bold witness; anyone can surrender to God to glorify God in all that we do	Ephesians 2:8-9, 2 Corinthians 12:8-9; Acts 9; Philippians 1:21; Philippians 4:13
Ruth	Excellence; hard work; nobility; loyalty; faithfulness	Ruth 3

Hannah	Faith; prayer; God doesn't forget anyone	1 Samuel 1; 1 Samuel 2:1-11
Mary of Bethany	Honoring God with all we have; devotion to God; friendship in Jesus	Matthew 26:6-13 John 11; John 12:1-8; Luke 10:38-42
Rahab	God rescues those who trust Him; faith in action	Joshua 2:1-24; Joshua 6
Esther	Courage, faithfulness, strength, and wisdom; each one of us has an important part of God's work in the world.	Esther; Esther 4:11-17
The lady who touched Jesus' cloak	Faith; determination; hope	Matthew 9:20-22

www.ingramcontent.com/pod-product-compliance
Lightning Source LLC
Chambersburg PA
CBHW042143290426
44110CB00002B/98